A History From Beginning to End

Copyright © 2017 by Hourly History.

All rights reserved.

Table of Contents

Introduction
Countdown to D-Day
Supreme Allied Commander Dwight D. Eisenhower
The Invasion Planning is Underway
A Day in June
The German Response
The Invasion
End Game

Introduction

D-Day, arguably the most significant military invasion of the twentieth century, doesn't have an authentic linguistic meaning. As Army jargon, D-Day was a term that first came into use in World War I on September 20, 1918, with the instructions that the First Army would attack at H-Hour on D-Day with the objective of forcing the evacuation of the salient at St. Mihiel. The days after a D-Day were indicated with a plus sign to indicate the precise day. That's the historical explanation of the term.

But not everyone agrees with that explanation. According to the French, the "D" stood for disembarkation or debarkation. Years later, when General Eisenhower's period of command and his two terms as president were over, his executive assistant responded to a letter asking the meaning of D-Day by writing that "any amphibious landing has a departure date; therefore, the shortened term D-Day is used." Furthermore, all the amphibious landings, whether at Sicily, North Africa, or the Pacific, had their own D-Day.

Whatever its origins, for most people, there is only one D-Day, and that's the one that took place on June 6, 1944, in Normandy. The invasion represented the first successful opposed landings to happen across the English Channel in more than eight centuries. But a lot had happened during the hundreds of years since that first invasion, and the players had changed significantly.

The attack would require a massive network of coordination of forces and supplies. There were a number of military leaders among the Allies who were men of the highest caliber of skill, men who had proven their mettle under fire in battle. Yet, when the time came to choose the one who would be the Supreme Allied Commander, the assignment was given to General Dwight David Eisenhower, a man who had served in the military for decades but had never fought in battle. He seemed, until World War II, to serve without distinction and as his career was winding down, there appeared little opportunity for advancement.

But just as World War II incubated people like Hitler, whose capacity for evil was enhanced by the centrifuge of war, so did it nurture men like Eisenhower, whose organizational talents, humble nature, and dedication to serve surfaced at a time when the world needed him. His skills had not been honed in hatred and vilification of other peoples, nor in arrogance of his own capacity, but in the routine duties of an officer in a peacetime army. He didn't have George Patton's fiery temperament or Bernard Montgomery's brilliance, but he was able to deal with them both, as well as with the churning developments that would take the Allied forces of freedom onto the shores of occupied Europe, to do battle against a menace that had brought the world into a long, dark night.

The planning required for such a campaign, almost cosmic in its duality of good and evil, was monumental. The land forces who came to invade were Americans,

British, Canadians, and Free French. Later, there would be Poles, Belgians, Czechs, Greeks, New Zealanders, Norwegians, Australians, and Dutch who would provide ground troops, along with air and naval support.

On the initial day of the invasion, over 160,000 Allied troops arrived along 50 miles of the French coastline; there were 5,000 ships and 13,000 aircraft. Their purpose was to bring the land war to Germany, to defeat the Nazis and liberate Europe from the evil that had conquered the continent under the twisted vision of Adolf Hitler.

It would not be an easy task, and victory was far from certain. But victory was all that the Allies could accept. Over 9,000 Allied soldiers were killed in the struggle to land on Nazi-occupied soil, but the landing was a success that allowed, by the time it was accomplished, more than 300,000 troops to gain hard-fought ground in Europe.

Chapter One

Countdown to D-Day

"This is no war of chieftains or of princes, of dynasties or national ambition; it is a war of peoples and of causes. There are vast numbers, not only in this Island but in every land, who will render faithful service in this war, but whose names will never be known, whose deeds will never be recorded. This is a War of the Unknown Warriors."

—Winston Churchill

The Allied invasion of Nazi-occupied Europe was a long time coming, and civilians and soldiers alike could be forgiven for wondering if the day would ever come when the scales of victory would begin to weigh in favor of the forces who found themselves in a global conflict against Germany. But despite the similarities in combatants and the brief intermission between World War I and World War II, the two confrontations were not the same.

That being said, many of the cast of characters remained the same. The War to End all Wars, as the First World War was idealistically titled, ended in 1918; the Second World War began on the calendar in 1939, although the sequence of victories and defeats, capitulation and genocide were not identical. In the eyes of many, the small number of years separating the end of

World War I and the onset of World War II was no more than an intermission which indicated that World War II was not a separate war at all.

The armistice that ended the First World War had given birth to an uneasy peace. The disillusioned youth who survived the first global conflict had their brief period of rebellion before the Great Depression burdened the population with an economic crisis so devastating that it crippled the world's markets, engendering mass unemployment that in turn led to social discontent and distrust in government.

In Germany, which was still paying for its culpability in starting World War I, the effects of Germany's disgrace, combined with its financial privations, inspired an unsuccessful Austrian artist to rebuild Aryan pride by tossing aside the terms of the Treaty of Versailles and dedicating himself to the restoration of German militarism and might. The rest of the world, consumed with its own problems, chose to ignore him. The boundaries of Germany increased with the annexation of the Austrian Anschluss, a region which Adolf Hitler, once a failed painter and now chancellor of Germany, claimed belonged to Germany because so many Germans lived there. As Jews, gypsies, homosexuals, and the handicapped were attacked, deprived of their rights and property, and finally taken away in railroad cars, never to be seen again, the world closed its eyes. Neville Chamberlain's "Peace for our time" announcement was later accused of appeasing Hitler, but in truth, Chamberlain likely realized that by accepting the Nazi annexation of the Anschluss, he had bought time for nations which needed to prepare for all-out war against an aggressive, advanced military power that has risen out of the ashes of the Treaty of Versailles.

By September 1939, the world could no longer close its eyes. Germany invaded Poland, swiftly conquering the unprepared country and beginning its conquest of Europe. France and Great Britain declared war on Germany. The United States chose neutrality, as it had at the beginning of World War I although President Franklin D. Roosevelt understood, as President Woodrow Wilson had not, that the United States would not be able to stay neutral in a world at war.

The so-called Phoney War ended in May 1940, as the German blitzkrieg invaded and defeated France, Belgium, the Netherlands, Norway, and Denmark, adding these countries like trophies to the national mantel.

With France occupied by the Nazis, Great Britain was on its own. Hitler was convinced that he would overpower the British with his Luftwaffe as the Battle of Britain commenced, but the Royal Air Force was able to prevent Hitler from invading the island nation. Hitler then invaded the Soviet Union, creating a two-front war which would, ultimately, be his undoing. Germany's roll call of conquest seemed likely to continue, but then, in December 1941, Germany gained an unexpected ally when the Empire of Japan attacked the American naval base at Pearl Harbor.

The sides had lined up: Germany, Italy, and Japan were the Axis Powers at war against the British, French, and the Americans and their allies. Although the United States had abstained from war until the Japanese attack, the agreed-upon strategy was "Europe First"; the first goal was the defeat of Germany. With that decision, the road to D-Day was marked.

Beginning in April 1942, Operation Bolero got underway as American forces headed to Great Britain for the preliminary stages of what would eventually be an invasion of Europe. At this stage, such an attempt would have been folly, as was evidenced by the deadly results when the Allies attacked Dieppe, France, suffering enormous casualties that indicated the carnage that the invasion would suffer. The effort was defeated by the Germans. Early in the war, the Germans seemed unstoppable.

But 1942 ended with some cause for optimism when General Bernard Montgomery defeated the Germans in the Battle of El Alamein in North Africa, which allowed British and American forces under the command of General Dwight D. Eisenhower to land in Morocco and Algeria. But the Allied leaders—Winston Churchill of Great Britain, Josef Stalin of the Soviet Union, and Franklin Roosevelt of the United States—knew that these victories were not enough to provide a solid foundation for an invasion. Meeting in Casablanca in January 1943, the Allies formed a staff charged with the initiation of a plan to invade Europe. D-Day was not yet a date on the calendar, but it was a date with destiny.

By March of that year, the British and Americans had begun planning an attack under the command of Great

Britain's Lieutenant-General Frederick E. Morgan. But the crucial role of the Supreme Allied Commander had not yet been filled. Who was the man best suited for this all-important role that would lead to the resolution of the war?

The leaders agreed to the outline that had been laid out for D-Day, and in October, the Allied naval commander for D-Day, Admiral Sir Bertram Ramsay, was named. Stalin was getting anxious and irritated at the delay in setting a date for the invasion of Europe. The Soviet Union was suffering on the Eastern Front, and Stalin needed the Allies to give the Germans something to worry about on their Western Front. They decided that the invasion would take place in May 1944.

The world knew an offensive was coming but didn't know when. Civilians wondered about their sons and husbands on the front. The German military leaders knew as well that their days as the masters of Europe might be numbered. Unless they stopped the invasion, their grand dreams of the Third Reich would crash in defeat, just as those dreams had died with the Treaty of Versailles after World War I. They were determined not to let that happen.

The Allied leader who would be given charge of the invasion bore a considerable amount of responsibility on his shoulders. The man who was chosen to be the Supreme Allied Commander was up to the challenge, although, to the undiscerning eye, he seemed to offer little in the way of qualifications for the position. Could so unassuming a man be the one who would lead the campaign to invade Europe and steal victory away from the arrogant Nazis? Dwight D. Eisenhower may not have been flashy, but his innate calm would be the trait that was needed to give the invasion its sense of possibility.

Chapter Two

Supreme Allied Commander Dwight D. Eisenhower

"A sense of humor is part of the art of leadership, of getting along with people, of getting things done."

—General Dwight D. Eisenhower

The man who was named Supreme Allied Commander had been an officer in the United States Army for 27 years. During those years, he had never been in combat. What was it about Dwight David Eisenhower that made him stand out among the potential candidates to be placed in charge of the largest invasion force the world had ever seen?

It was not his academic prowess at West Point. The class of 1915 would yield 59 generals out of its 164 graduates, but Eisenhower's rank was 61st academically and 125th in discipline. But what he did excel at was organization, and his superior officers soon noticed this talent. After the United States entered World War I in 1917, Eisenhower was appointed to command a tank training center. As a young army officer, Eisenhower knew that he needed to serve on the battle field if he wanted to be promoted, and he was hopeful that this chance had arrived in October 1918, when he was instructed to go to France with his unit. But on November 11, 1918, the armistice was signed. The war was over, and with it, Eisenhower feared, his chance of advancement in his career.

But there was work in a peacetime army as well, and Eisenhower served where he was sent. He was a major when he graduated first among 275 others from the Command and General Staff School. A posting to France followed and in 1928, Eisenhower graduated from the Army War College, again ranking first. He was an aide to General Douglas MacArthur, serving with him in the Philippines until 1939. His ascent up the ladder of rank was slow and plodding, but in every posting, Eisenhower proved that he had a rare gift for planning and organization. Those talents, unheralded upon the battle field, were crucial if victory was ever to come to the Allied cause.

Throughout the 1920s and 1930s, Eisenhower must have appeared to be the classic example of the mundane military man without much in the way of dash or brilliance. After 25 years in the army, he would not rise to the rank of colonel until 1940. But from his earliest days as a West Point cadet, he had won the admiration of those around him for his ability to mediate disputes and to work with others toward achieving a shared goal. Throughout his years of service, he continued to strive to better his knowledge so that, if called upon, he could perform his best.

During that time, Franklin D. Roosevelt recognized what his fellow Americans did not want to admit, and as president, it was his job to ready a reluctant country for war. Such a war would take a monumental effort on the part of the Americans, who were by no means eager for the conflict.

Eisenhower's talents had been noticed by the exacting, discerning Army Chief of Staff General George Marshall, who appointed him to the War Plans Division in Washington D.C. to work on the strategy for the invasion of Europe. Eisenhower was part of that preparation as the army expanded its forces. In September 1941, Eisenhower was promoted to the rank of brigadier general. Three months later, five days after the Japanese bombed Pearl Harbor and the United States entered the war, General Marshall sent word that he needed to see Eisenhower immediately. He asked Eisenhower how he thought the strategy of the Pacific campaign ought to be outlined.

A few hours later, Eisenhower presented Marshall with a brief, succinct response. Marshall already knew what he wanted to do in the Pacific; the assignment to Eisenhower was a test. Marshall said, "The Department is filled with able men who analyze their problems well but feel compelled always to bring them to me for final solution." What Marshall needed, he said, was "assistants who will solve their own problems and tell me later what they have done."

Operation Torch was the Allied invasion of French North Africa and Eisenhower, now a lieutenant general, was in charge of it. He proved his mettle as commander of Operation Torch, where he designed a smooth-operating system of unified command that earned the respect of the British and Canadian subordinates under him. The invasion of Tunisia, Sicily, and the Italian mainland was successful.

The British military leadership, as well as Churchill, felt that they had more combat experience than the Americans. The American soldiers were novices, and although Roosevelt agreed with Stalin that the invasion of Europe should begin sooner, the British were aware that the Americans weren't yet ready to go up against the hardened, experienced Nazi army. An invasion of Europe in 1943, when there would not be enough American soldiers on hand to make a difference, could have been a devastating failure. And this was a mission that could not fail.

Because the Americans would be energizing the fighting with their forces and weapons, and because one person needed to be in command of the operation, the British knew that the United States would claim the role. Roosevelt's choice for the assignment was Marshall, but the British didn't agree, and in any case, Marshall was performing excellently as the Army's Chief of Staff where his assignment was to build the army and allocate the resources it needed.

But Eisenhower had appeal. He wasn't a showboat like Great Britain's Bernard Montgomery, and he wasn't temperamental like America's George Patton. Eisenhower was easy to work with while maintaining a firm command; he was judicious and got along with the other nationalities under his command. If the invasion was to succeed, Eisenhower, along with everyone else in the military, realized that someone needed to be assigned to oversee all the United States' operations in Europe. But he did not expect to be the person named to the position. His superior officer proved otherwise, and in December 1943, Marshall selected Eisenhower over 366 senior officers as Supreme Allied Commander of the Allied Expeditionary Force. To him would fall the responsibility of planning Operation Overlord, the largest combined land, air, and sea military operation in history.

The British had a presence among the leadership; Air Marshal Sir Arthur Tedder would be named as the Deputy Supreme Commander. Montgomery too, had a primary role, although not the role he might have coveted. "Monty" was appointed to command the 21st Army Group, in charge of the D-Day assault landings and the ground fighting that would follow.

The New Year dawned with the knowledge that, in a few months, all the planning would be tested. Another welcome event happened in the first month when, on January 27, after close to 900 days under siege, the city of Leningrad was freed. Nearly one million of the city's residents had died from the unrelenting shelling, starvation, or disease. The German had suffered too from the siege, and their ranks had been depleted. Soldiers who needed a respite from the grueling effects of serving on the Eastern Front were often sent to the Western Front, where so far, nothing much was going on. The invasion loomed, but nothing was definite yet.

Settling on May 31 as the designated date for the attack, the commanders realized that more troops needed to land in the first wave of the invasion, and more troops meant that more support would be needed from air and naval forces. There was still much to arrange if the invasion would have any hope of succeeding, and failure was not an option. As the days fell away upon the calendar, Eisenhower's superb planning skills were put to the ultimate test.

Chapter Three

The Invasion Planning is Underway

"Plans are nothing; planning is everything."

—General Dwight D. Eisenhower

England's history had benefitted from its English Channel as the Spanish Empire's Armada during the time of Elizabeth I and the French under Napoleon had found it unassailable. But now, it was the boundary between the Allies and their target.

Hitler, determined to keep the Allied forces from reaching his acquired empire, had ordered the building of the Atlantic Wall in his Directive 51. The Atlantic Wall was fortified with barbed wire and tank top turrets, and mines to prevent the Allies from advancing once the invasion came. Hitler was convinced that the landings would take place at high tide, and with that in mind, he had ordered these fortifications to obstruct landing vessels. Knowing that Hitler expected the invasion at high tide was valuable information for the Allies, who based their timing upon low tide as a result.

Germany was well aware that the Allies were planning to invade Europe. In December 1943, Field Marshal Erwin

Rommel was assigned to bolster the German defenses with minefields, pillboxes, and obstacles to sink the landing craft along the French coast. Rommel, a German officer steeped in the military tradition, was given the task of finishing the 2,400-mile Atlantic Wall, which stretched from western France to Norway. The building of the Atlantic Wall had begun in 1942. However, only the major parts could be considered well defended, and only the Pas-de-Calais could claim an unending chain of defense. Upon his appointment to the position, Rommel called for a significant build-up of the fortifications that were in place with the addition of gun emplacements, beach obstacles, pillboxes, and millions of mines.

The same kind of work was underway along the English coasts, as huge artificial harbors made of steel and concrete, known as Mulberry harbors, were being built so that, after the invasion, they could be brought to Normandy and assembled. Their purpose was to provide the forces with the ability to swiftly land and unload soldiers and equipment rather than doing so right on the beaches.

In order to strengthen the Allied forces for the invasion, it was necessary to bring the war to Germany. As the Allies began to bomb German cities in 1944, Germans retaliated with its "Little Blitz," a bombing campaign of England that was less devastating than the Blitz of 1940-1941. Hitler and his cadre of leaders had long been furious at the fact that Great Britain had withstood the original Blitz and now that the planning for the invasion was taking place on English soil, Hitler was even more incensed. He looked forward to the invasion so that Germany would have the opportunity to defeat the English once and for all.

It was up to Eisenhower and his staff to predict the Nazi response and foil it, while undertaking the phenomenal amount of work that the Allied invasion would require. That planning required stealth and skill. As early as January 1944, midget submarines covertly went to Normandy to obtain samples of the sand, so that the Allies could guarantee that the landing beaches would be able to support the weight of the tanks that would land. Allied aircraft began dropping supplies, including weapons, to support the French Resistance so that, after the invasion was underway, the French would have the means to battle the occupying Nazi regime.

In February, the Royal Air Force and the United States 8th Air Force led a series of raids on cities in Germany. German planes defended the homeland, but the losses to both civilians and pilots took its toll, and the Germans felt the loss in their numbers which were not easy to replace. This depletion of men and aircraft would have an effect on Germany's ability to defend against the invasion when it commenced.

Once the plans were in place, it was time for the Allied senior officers to draw up their own tactics to oversee the actual landing of the brigades, regiments, and battalions, even though the soldiers were not yet told when or where the invasion was going to happen.

A training exercise called Exercise Tiger in late April was a reminder of how deadly the invasion would be, when Americans were intercepted by the German E-boats on Slapton Sands, Devon. More than 600 Americans were killed, and three of the landing ship tanks or LSTs, which were capable of carrying as many as 70 armored vehicles, were sunk or damaged. The casualties were another reminder of the caliber of the enemy that the Allies faced, and Hitler was convinced that his superior soldiers would defeat the inferior foes.

What Hitler could not defend against was the skill and good fortune of the intelligence that the Allies were receiving, and the duplicity of the counterintelligence they were sending to the Nazis. The elite German troops were stationed at the Pas-de-Calais because of Hitler's belief that this was the target point of the invasion; they would stay there, and not be in Normandy, until July. When German reconnaissance flights flew over the island of Great Britain, they were duped by the staged areas designed to fool the Nazis.

While preparing to invade Normandy, the Allies hoped to deceive Hitler into believing that the main thrust of the invasion was at Pas-de-Calais, the narrowest point between Great Britain and France. The fraudulent invasion included a fake army based in Great Britain under the command of General George Patton. The skullduggery involved in the campaign of deception included fraudulent radio transmissions and double agents.

So fragile was the secrecy of the invasion date that officers who knew when D-Day was scheduled had a special code name. They were called "Bigot" derived from "to Gibraltar" which was the destination stamped on the official papers of the officers who had participated in the invasion of North Africa in 1942. These officers were not sent anywhere where there was a chance that they would be captured, in order to preserve the information from leaking out.

Some of the Bigots were among the missing when Germans attacked Americans LSTs who were participating in Exercise Tiger. Had the fate of the Bigots not been learned, the invasion would have been canceled. Every effort was made to learn the whereabouts of the missing ten, and when the bodies were recovered, the plans for the invasion remained intact.

But knowledge did leak out, unfortunately. The Germans managed to obtain some documents referring to Overlord, but the documents didn't include the relevant details needed to unravel the riddle of where the invasion would take place. A Spanish double agent named Juan Pujol, who had moved to England in order to pretend to spy for the Germans, was able to convince Hitler and his military leaders that Normandy was no more than a diversionary tactic to lure the Germans away from Pas-de-Calais.

Some leaks came, unwittingly, through the Allied side and when they happened, Eisenhower's response was swift and severe. Major General Henry Miller, the United States 9th Air Force's chief supply officer, shared his woes about the supply problems he was having with guests at a party in London; the problems would ease after the invasion, which, he informed his fellow guests, was going to happen before June 15. When Eisenhower learned of the leak, Miller was demoted to the rank of lieutenant colonel and sent back to the United States in disgrace.

What neither leaks nor planning could alter was the weather, upon which the actual date of the invasion was depending. After May was abandoned as a choice, two periods of time in June were deemed suitable due to the amount of moonlight that would be available from June 5 to 7 and June 18 to 20. June 5 was looking like the ideal date.

Early in May, the final series of training exercise began along England's southern coast. Named Exercise Fabius, the endeavor landed 25,000 troops at different beaches and ended on May 8. On May 13, Prime Minister Winston Churchill and King George VI went to St. Paul's School to attend the final briefing for the senior officers. The troops who would be landing in Normandy were encamped along England's southern coast, and by the end of May, the camps would be sealed to prevent news from leaking out to the public that the invasion was about to take place. Waterproofing of the vehicles that would be wading through the deep water was accomplished. Because of the size of the embarkation, the process would take place over five days. On May 31, the first wave of troops began loading onto the vessels and landing craft heading to Normandy.

Chapter Four

A Day in June

"You are about to embark upon the Great Crusade, toward which we have striven these many months. The eyes of the world are upon you."

—General Dwight D. Eisenhower

Meteorology was an inescapable player in the planning for D-Day. The date chosen needed to be near the full moon, both for lighting up the landmarks so that the aircraft, glider, and landing craft could see well enough to navigate and for the spring tide so that the defensive obstacles put in place by the Germans would be visible as the Allies approached the beaches. June 6 would have a full moon, leading General Eisenhower to schedule June 5 as D-Day for the invasion.

On the first day of June 1944, Eisenhower's headquarters was moved to Southwick House north of Portsmouth. By this time, nerves were on edge and every event, however innocuous, was interpreted as a breach of security. On that Thursday, one of the clues in the *Daily Telegraph* crossword puzzle was "Neptune." That would have seemed harmless, except for the fact that Neptune was a code word for the naval crossing. Upon investigation, it was learned that the puzzle had been created months before by a school headmaster in Surrey who had no prior knowledge of the invasion that loomed.

But on the evening of the same date, the BBC broadcast lines from a Paul Verlaine poem, which was a coded warning for the French Resistance regarding its plans for a railway sabotage, meaning that the invasion was due to take place within a month. German intelligence, which was monitoring the broadcast, intercepted the message and knew that it applied to the invasion plans. An alert was sent to the German 15th Army which was based in northern France, but the German 7th Army, which was the force that was based in Normandy, was not forewarned.

The first American and British airborne troops, the first Allied soldiers who would land in Normandy, began to take off from England around 11:00 pm; they would arrive in Normandy by glider and parachute early the next morning.

Two Royal Navy mini-submarines, the first round of departures for the invasion fleet, set off on June 2. They arrived a day later and, like so many others, prepared to wait. Their role was to remain under water until the invasion when they would surface and guide the Allied craft at Juno and Sword Beaches. The warships which would begin the bombardment of the German defenses on D-Day departed from Belfast, the Clyde, and Scapa Flow.

Early on the morning of June 3, the weather forecast brought bad news for June 5. The next day's weather did not look promising and at 4:15 am, the decision was made to postpone the invasion. The wind and the high seas meant that larger ships wouldn't be able to launch their landing craft. The low clouds would be an obstacle for the aircraft seeking their targets.

The threat of bad weather jeopardized the entire operation; if the invasion had to be canceled, the nearly impossible task of returning the soldiers to their embarkation camps would be required, a daunting assignment, considering that troops were already on their way. Waiting would take at least a month until the next full moon came.

But ultimately, the weather would have the last say about when the invasion could take place. Those ships that had been sent forward anticipating a June 5 attack were called back, taking shelter along Great Britain's southern coast in the bays and inlets for the night.

It was good news for the Germans. Aware of the forecast and knowing that the weather was even worse in the north of France than it was over the English Channel, Erwin Rommel headed home to Germany to celebrate his wife's birthday with the intention of returning on June 8, although he doubted that the weather would cooperate in time for the invasion to take place.

Field Marshal Erwin Rommel was a formidable opponent. He had won the respect of his enemies for his bravery and his brilliance in battle during the North Africa campaign, where he had earned the nickname "Desert Fox." In 1942, he was promoted to the rank of field marshal following his victory over the British at Gazala and the taking of Tobruk. Ultimately, however, the Allies were victorious in North Africa, and in 1943,

Rommel returned to Europe. In 1944, he was placed in command of Army Group B in northwest Europe. He was convinced that for Germany to be victorious over the Allied invasion, the Germans had to be prepared along the coast in order to counteract the advantages of the Allied airpower. Rommel was a realist. Large scale armored counter operations following the allied landing upon the coast would be futile because of the effectiveness of the Allied air battle. Therefore, Rommel felt that the goal should be to thwart the invasion so that the Germans could negotiate peace in the west and concede to a stalemate in the east. His view, regarded as pessimism by Hitler and his circle, would ultimately cost him his life when the Third Reich began to crumble and scapegoats were needed to take the blame.

But in the meantime, the invasion seemed to be off for now. Other German senior officers left for the weekend and some commanders, still practicing at war games to prepare for the invasion, were not at their posts.

Germany thought the invasion was postponed, but the media of the Allied nations were alert to any news, and they were practicing for the attack. The teletype operator for the Associated Press, unaware that the report was live, announced that the invasion had begun. That particular bit of breaking news captured the world's notice until, five minutes later, AP issued a correction. Everyone was on tenterhooks, waiting for the latest bit of news to come out, all realizing that it was weather that would decide.

Weather is fickle. On the evening of June 4, during a meeting with meteorologist Group Captain J.M. Stagg,

Eisenhower learned that there would be an improvement of the weather in 36 hours. Eisenhower, along with General Bernard Montgomery wanted to move ahead with D-Day on June 6. Air Chief Marshal Leigh Mallory was less enthusiastic. Commander-in-Chief Admiral Bertram Ramsay felt that the odds of success were slightly in the Allies' favor. It was enough to convince Eisenhower to move forward with the invasion. D-Day was set for June 6. The work of painting black and white stripes on the Allied aircraft got underway; the purpose was to help the Allies recognize each other. With the green light signaling go for the invasion, junior officers started opening their sealed orders to find out where they were going to land.

But the preparation was not yet finished. The soldiers received their order of the day for June 6, 1944, from General Eisenhower. "The eyes of the world are upon you," he told them. "The hopes and prayers of liberty-loving people everywhere march with you." Their mission, he said, was to bring about the destruction of the German war machine, the elimination of Nazi tyranny over the oppressed peoples of Europe, and security for Americans in a free world. Eisenhower did not pretend that the mission would be easy. Acknowledging the training and experience of the Germany military, Eisenhower reminded them that the Allies had turned the tide of war and reduced the ability of the Nazis to overcome superior forces. The Allies, he said, would accept nothing less than full victory; he had complete confidence in their courage, their devotion to duty, and their skill in battle.

Despite his confidence in his forces, Eisenhower knew that victory was not guaranteed. With that in mind, he had a second message ready in case the invasion failed; the letter explained his decision to attack, based on the information that was available at the time. In this second prepared message, he praised the troops for their bravery and devotion to duty. If the mission failed, Eisenhower shouldered the onus. "If any blame or fault attaches to the attempt it is mine alone."

Chapter Five

The German Response

"Make peace, you idiots!"

—Field Marshal Gerd von Rundstedt

The year 1944 was the high-point for the Germany military in terms of the forces it could summon. The Eastern Front had over 5,000 tanks, and the Luftwaffe had more than 5,000 aircraft. On June 6, 1944, there were 157 German divisions in the Soviet Union, 59 in France, Belgium, and the Netherlands, 21 in the Balkans, and smaller numbers stationed in Finland, Norway, Denmark, and Germany. However, German records show that before the invasion, the actual numbers were at 50% of their personnel. The Allied Air Forces had not been idle as Eisenhower prepared for the invasion and they had launched strikes against Germany which required the Luftwaffe to pull resources from other locations in order to defend the home front. The depletion of men and aircraft would diminish the Nazi defense against the invasion.

But Hitler had made it clear that the enemy was not to advance into Europe. On November 3, 1943, he had issued Führer Directive No. 51, which threatened deadly consequences should the Allies be able to claim a foothold onto the continent. His strategy was to throw the Allies back into the sea with a mighty counter-attack after reinforcing his defenses along the west.

Hitler failed to realize that the crack Nazi troops were not located in the western regions of his conquered lands. In fact, the troops that had fought on the Eastern Front were sent to the west so that they could recover from the brutal fighting they had experienced.

But Hitler's will was not to be disobeyed, and by the end of May 1944, 58 German divisions out of the total of 300, were sent to France, Belgium, and the Netherlands.

Both Hitler and Joseph Goebbels, the Nazi propaganda minister, wanted the invasion to take place; otherwise, they reasoned, Germany would continue to watch and wait, leading to a decline in Germany's resources. The increase in Allied bombings had begun to threaten the availability of gasoline for the Nazi vehicles, and if the waiting endured for too long, the Allies could gain the upper hand. While the Allies were based in England, they were out of reach of the German military machine. But with an invasion, they would be targets.

Field Marshal Erwin Rommel was the commander of Army Group B, which consisted of Germany's 7th Army in Normandy and Brittany, the 15th Army located in the Pas-de-Calais, which the Germans believed was the target of the invasion, and the LXXXVIII Corps in the Netherlands. Field Marshal Gerd von Rundstedt, the commander of the forces in western Europe, could also call upon the 1st and 19th Armies, or Group G, giving him 50 infantry and 10 Panzer divisions.

Von Rundstedt was a veteran of World War I who had retired in 1938 but returned to active service when World War II broke out. After taking part in the conquering of Poland, he was instrumental in defeating France in 1940 in the early days of the war. He was impressive in command of the German southern wing of the invasion of the Soviet Union, which began in June 1941 and by December had won control of most of Ukraine. But when the Soviet counteroffensive forced a German retreat, von Rundstedt was dismissed from command. He returned to duty in June 1942 as commander-in-chief in western Europe, where he immediately began the work of defending France against the inevitable invasion by the Allies.

Because he realized that the Allies would own the air, Rommel wanted to have the armored formations deployed close to the beaches where the invasion was going to take place. Specifically, he said that one Panzer division on the first day was preferable to three on the third day after the Allies had already established a presence. Internal squabbles were also affecting the German military. General Leo Geyr von Schweppenburg, known as von Geyr, and Rommel were in discord regarding the most efficient deployment of the Panzer divisions.

Von Geyr, following the traditional policy, said the Panzers would be concentrated around the cities of Paris and Rouen, to be deployed when the main Allied beachhead had been identified. When Hitler had been consulted for his opinion, he decreed that Rommel would get three Panzer divisions and the remainder would be in the Oberkommando der Wehrmacht (OKW) or High Command of the Armed Forces, which claimed oversight, at least nominally, of the Germany Army, Navy, and Air Force. Of these divisions, only three would be deployed where they would be close enough to react to an invasion of northern France; the remaining four were sent to the Netherlands and the south of France. Only Hitler had the authority to command the OKW divisions and send them into action or move them.

Still convinced that the actual attack was to take place at Pas-de-Calais, the German High Command would not give Field Marshal Gerd von Rundstedt permission to commit the armored reserves until later on June 6, by which time they were destined to be less successful. OKW dealt imperiously with the German commanders and challenged the decisions that they made; Hitler, when approached by the commanders for more authority, refused. Von Rundstedt would be removed from command by the end of June for telling Field Marshal Keitel, the Chief of Staff at the Armed Forces Headquarters, to "make peace, you idiots."

Not all of the problems faced by the Germans had to do with discord among the officers. Communication was compromised because of the effectiveness of the Allied air and naval superiority. The Germans would soon find their mobility crippled by the air-power of the Allies, as bridges were destroyed and the Germans had no choice but to take detours.

The Allied Navy was also diligent in protecting the troops as they advanced. Defense upon the beach was a challenge for the local German commanders, a problem that Rommel had foreseen. But all ranks saw a failure to respond effectively and swiftly to the assault. Although the German forces were capably led by the experienced Rommel and von Rundstedt, they lacked the authority to counter the voice of Hitler, who believed that he knew more than his generals. The error of his belief would cost the Third Reich dearly.

Chapter Six

The Invasion

"The waiting for history to be made was the most difficult. I spent much time in prayer. Being cooped up made it worse. Like everyone else, I was seasick and the stench of vomit permeated our craft."

—Private Clair Galdonik

By the time dawn broke on the morning of June 6, there were already Allied forces behind enemy lines. Paratroopers and glider troops were on the ground with the task of securing bridges and exit roads. The morning had started early for one British and two American airborne divisions, which had been dropped behind the beaches at 2:00 am, parachuting in so that they could designate the zones and secure the routes for the forces coming from the water. The British troops captured the bridges at Benouville and Ranville which were located to the east of the landing beaches. The navy and air forces began a fierce bombardment to prepare the way for more than 5,000 ships and 4,000 ship-to-shore craft, which began to land at 6:30 am.

That was the time when the actual amphibious invasion commenced. For the Canadians and British who were capturing Gold, Juno, and Sword Beaches, the

Germans proved to be minimal threats. The same was true for the Americans aiming for Utah Beach. But it was a different story for the Americans aiming for Omaha Beach, where the opposition was heavy and American casualties numbered around 2,000.

The Germans, completely duped by the successful efforts of the Allies to make them believe that the invasion was aiming for the Pas-de-Calais, woke up on June 6 to see that 50 miles of the coast of Normandy was crowded with nearly 7,000 ships.

The Germans had placed most of their Panzer divisions north and east of the Seine, making them unavailable to help at Normandy. The surprise at the site of the invasion was compounded by the mayhem caused by the Allied aircraft, which were dropping troops at a swift and dizzying pace. The Germans lacked air reconnaissance; corps, division, and regimental commanders were in Rennes at the war games; ironically, they were practicing for the invasion. Because the Luftwaffe no longer ruled the skies, it would have been too dangerous for Field Marshal Rommel to fly back to Normandy as soon as he learned of the invasion, with the result that he spent June 6 on the road, driving back to La Roche-Guyon.

The Allies had their personality frictions, but nothing like what was going on in the German High Command. Hitler had no faith in the military leaders, and they certainly didn't trust him.

The soldier who did follow orders and was able to keep his head was Field Marshal Gerd Rundstedt, the World

War I veteran who had been mocked by Hitler and the OKW as an aging, out-of-touch remnant of a failed war. Sensing that the airborne landings could not possibly be a decoy because of the numbers and that they would have to be reinforced from the water, von Rundstedt ordered the two reserve Panzer divisions that were available in Normandy to move without delay toward Caen. When the attack came, von Rundstedt wanted armored units to be there to meet them.

Because Hitler did not authorize them to move, the commanders of these Panzer divisions were unable to be of use on D-Day. Unfortunately for the German counterattack, those divisions were under the command of the OKW, which refused von Rundstedt's request (made after he had already ordered the division to move, because the pragmatic officer knew there was no time to lose) to send them to Caen. The divisions could not be moved until the Fuhrer gave the command, and Hitler was still asleep. So von Rundstedt had to countermand his earlier order until Hitler awoke. Even when the commanders requested permission, Hitler's staff refused to wake him when they learned that the invasion was underway.

When Hitler awoke at noon, he authorized the divisions to move, but by then, the cloud cover had dissipated and the Allied aircraft were in the air, striking at anything in motion on the ground below. The divisions hid in the woods, waiting for the evening so that they could continue to move under the protection of darkness.

Gleeful that the Allies were finally out in the open, Hitler was confident that the British were in position for their destruction by the German forces. Of course, he was also convinced that the invasion had been at Pas-de-Calais, pointing to the location on a map as he and Goebbels conferred. Goebbels did not refute the error.

Eager to retaliate against the Allies, Hitler ordered a bombing raid on London on June 6 after the invasion began. This was to be the unveiling of a new weapon, the V-1, a jet-powered plan that carried a one-ton warhead. However, not only was the plane's targeting inaccurate, only hitting its London targets 20 percent of the time, but Hitler had failed to consider the amount of time needed to put his orders into practice. The planes could not immediately be sent into action, and the attack didn't begin until June 12. Of the ten that were sent out, four crashed right away, three hit open fields, two disappeared, and one destroyed a railway bridge. As a means for venting Hitler's rage, the planes may have been a success, but in terms of retaliating against the Allies, they did not affect the outcome of the invasion.

Hitler would have been enraged to realize how successfully the invasion was proceeding for the Allies. After establishing the beachhead, two artificial Mulberry harbors were brought over from England in segments. One was put in place at Arromanches by the British, and the other was placed at Omaha Beach by the Americans. The artificial harbors were operational by June 9. Until it was destroyed by storms on June 19, the Omaha Beach Mulberry harbor would facilitate the landing of more than

314,000 men, 41,000 vehicles, and 116,000 tons of supplies. The Arromanches Mulberry harbor was equally successful, with 9,000 tons of supplies landing daily until the end of August.

But by that time, with the securing of the port of Cherbourg, the Allies were no longer dependent upon the artificial harbors. By the end of June, the Allies had seized the vital port of Cherbourg, landed approximately 850,000 men and 150,000 vehicles in Normandy, and were en route to proceed with the liberation of France.

But not all plans went as swiftly or smoothly as originally expected. The Allies had intended to capture Saint-Lô , Caen, and Bayeux on the first day of the invasion so that all of the beaches except Utah and Sword would be connected. Plans also included establishing a front line of six to ten miles from the beach. But seven Panzer divisions were in the way of that goal and it took the British and Canadians six weeks to capture Caen. The Americans advanced more swiftly, with only two Panzer divisions between them and their destination.

By June 11, the beaches had been completely secured. Casualties numbered over 10,000, which, although enormous, were less than the 20,000 that Winston Churchill had expected. The victory was not yet won, but with 326,000 Allied troops, 50,000 vehicles, and 100,000 tons of equipment, Europe could foresee a dawning when the Nazi flag would be lowered and their countries would be free again.

But the Germans had no intention of giving up without a relentless fight to retain the European soil they had won. They had lost World War I, but they were not reconciled to the notion that defeat awaited them in this Second World War.

Chapter Seven

End Game

"There is one great thing that you men will all be able to say after this war is over and you are home once again. You may be thankful that twenty years from now when you are sitting by the fireplace with your grandson on your knee and he asks you what you did in the great World War II, you won't have to cough, shift him to the other knee and say, 'Well, your Granddaddy shoveled shit in Louisiana.'"

—General George S. Patton, Jr.

The summer of 1944 may be unique in the history of military exploits. By the time that June ended, the Allied forces had managed to transport almost one million men and more than 585,000 tons of supplies over the beaches where they had launched the invasion. But the Germans had made the Allies fight for every inch of land they reclaimed.

Field Marshal Rommel had begun the war loyal to Adolf Hitler. By 1944, he realized that the volatile German leader was unable or unwilling to understand the situation in concrete terms. Rommel understood, as Hitler refused to, that Germany which was fighting a two-front war after the successful invasion on D-Day could not win either conflict. But when he tried to convince

Hitler of the facts, Hitler refused to accept Rommel's words.

Rommel decided that he would surrender the German forces in the west, on his own, without Hitler's authorization. But after he was wounded in an air attack in July, he was forced to return home. On October 14, Hitler sent messengers with two choices for Rommel: he could either choose to be charged with high treason and go on trial or he could commit suicide. Because the latter option meant that his family would be immune from his disgrace and because his death would be attributed to a heart attack, Rommel chose suicide. He was honored with a state funeral at his death.

Normandy was not the only invasion that summer. Another invasion, this one in the south of France, was codenamed Operation Dragoon and began on August 15. The Battle of Normandy, as the June 6 invasion was called, ended when the Germans were forced out of northwest France. When August was over, the two million Allied troops had liberated Paris and were on their way to Germany. The Allies were advancing from the west, the Soviets from the east, with the intention of meeting in Germany.

Hitler needed every man in uniform to protect Germany, which meant that he was powerless to send any of his troops in France to buttress the Eastern Front against the advancing Soviet troops, who bore no love for the Germans after the carnage the Russian people had endured.

Because of his failure to repulse the Allied advance, von Rundstedt had been replaced in July. However, he was called back into service to conduct the Battle of the Bulge. In March 1945, he was once again removed from command. American forces captured him in May but released him because of illness.

On April 30, 1945, Adolf Hitler committed suicide. On May 8, Germany surrendered unconditionally.

On the 65th anniversary of D-Day, American President Barack Obama noted that the efforts of the soldiers who participated in the invasion of Normandy changed the course of history. "It was unknowable then," Obama said, "but so much of the progress that would define the twentieth century, on both sides of the Atlantic, came down to the battle for a slice of beach only six miles long and two miles wide." Had the effort failed, Obama went on to say, Hitler's death grip on Europe could have gone on indefinitely.

The victory was an Allied effort, and praise belongs to all who took part in the endeavor. The Herculean labors of launching so massive an invasion against a powerful and determined enemy, in a challenging landscape during uncooperative weather must be regarded as a human triumph. Credit must also be given to the determined, hardworking, unassuming Supreme Allied Commander General Dwight D. Eisenhower, who did not allow the obstacles he faced to deter his determination to succeed. He remained faithful to the broad definition of the strategy that he had outlined before the invasion, but he showed himself willing and able to change tactics when change was necessary for victory to take place.

In 1947, General Eisenhower appeared before a group of 165 student journalists. When asked what the greatest decision he had had to make during the war was, Eisenhower began to pace in front of the students, his hands clasped behind his back as he formed his answer. He told the students that, on May 30, a close friend and a trusted aide, later identified as British Air Chief Marshal Sir Trafford Leigh-Mallory, the air commander of the invasion, came to see Eisenhower late at night. He explained that, again and again, he had considered the prospects and had determined that the invasion could not succeed. Casualties to the glider troops would be 90% before they reached land; the rate of death and wounded for the paratroopers would be 75%. By that estimate, too many men would be casualties, leaving too few able to fulfill their mission. Eisenhower, respecting the judgment of his fellow officer, agreed to think over what he had said.

The numbers were alarming, and the prospect of losing over 13,000 soldiers was sobering. But if the Allies could not seize and hold the causeways, the Germans would control the strips of land that the Allies needed if they were going to reach the mainland. Eisenhower reviewed the planning, but the inescapable fact remained if the airborne troops were unable to secure the causeways, there was no hope for the soldiers who were risking their lives by landing on the beaches.

Eisenhower let the order stand. He told the students, "The airborne boys did their job."

That is the lesson of D-Day. The Allied forces did their job and, in so doing, they unleashed the tide of liberty across Europe, bringing the nightmare of Nazism to a hard-fought end. Today, the swastika stands as a despised symbol of hatred and oppression. Germany is a progressive and influential force for freedom in Europe, a nation committed to preventing a recurrence of that bitter episode in its past. Europe, once a bloody patchwork of combative nations, is united with common goals. The world, despite all its problems, has come a long way, thanks to that slice of beach six miles long and two miles wide.

Made in United States
North Haven, CT
17 September 2023

41658257R00026